IN SEARCH OF PEACE AND BELONGING
Through Letter Writing

by

Francine Beauvoir, PhD

With Foreword

by

Andrea and Bob Kamm
Los Osos, California, February 2019

The cover painting entitled *"En chemin vers la lumiere"*
is owned by Francine and Bruce Crapuchettes
and was purchased from the painter Jacqueline Olivier
in the quaint village of Barbizon near Paris, France
on October 1, 2017.

Jacqueline Olivier has given permission for us to use her
painting for the cover of this book.

IN SEARCH OF PEACE AND BELONGING THROUGH LETTER WRITING

Library of Congress Cataloging-in-Publication Data

Beauvoir, PhD, Francine C.

IN SEARCH OF PEACE AND BELONGING THROUGH LETTER WRITING

ISBN

Library of Congress Control Number: 2016921446
CreateSpace Independent Publishing Platform
North Charleston, South Carolina

Also by Francine Beauvoir:

Raising Cooperative & Self-Confident Children: A Step-By-Step Guide For Conscious Parenting

By Francine Beauvoir and Bruce Crapuchettes:

An Imago Clinical Handbook: 300 Questions Answered From 20 Years Of Training Psychotherapists In Imago Relationship Therapy

Getting Back The Love We Had: Forty-Two Answers To Real Questions From Couples Who Feared They Were Losing Their Way

Volume One - Ending The Power Struggle

Volume Two - Rebuilding Our Dream

Volume Three - A New Focus On Each Other

To

All the clients I have helped over the years
to write letters in order to find peace
and belonging. I am very grateful
to have had the opportunity
to work together
with them.

Table of Contents

Acknowledgements

First and foremost, I am very grateful to all the clients who have allowed me to publish the letters we have worked on together. I want to acknowledge their willingness to be guided away from vengeance and toward Peace and Belonging. They have won an enormous battle with their ego. Together, we paved the way toward a gentler world. My deepest appreciations and congratulations!

Thank you to my faithful husband who has typed and re-typed and typed some more for me. Typing is not one of my strengths, and knowing that I can count on him, totally alleviated my practical concerns. Brucie, you are my champion!

I also thank Jacqueline Olivier, a marvelous painter whose gallery is in the quaint artist village of Barbizon near Paris, France, who give us written permission to use her painting for our cover.

My deepest thanks also to Bob and Andrea Kamm, both successful therapists, writers and authors, who read the first rendering of this work. They were encouraging as well as enlightening through their astute suggestions – a balance I really appreciated. Bob is an outstanding editor and Andrea the perfect complement. A living example of the notion that one plus one equals more than two! You were the gentle nudge I needed to pursue this work.

Foreword

We have been professional colleagues with Francine for many years and have always been touched by her command of her subject matter, her clarity, creativity, generosity and personal warmth. All these qualities are evident in this current book, particularly in the way Francine so carefully yet forthrightly guides her clients to find new ways of expressing themselves that are true and honest without becoming ensnared in old blame and shame traps.

Francine and her husband and partner, Bruce, have long had a bedrock commitment to clinical excellence in their practice of Imago Relationship Therapy. This book is an expression of that commitment in that it represents an important contribution to the literature of therapeutic practice, specifically Imago therapeutic practice. The use of letter writing to facilitate healing and growth has been around for a long time.

Yet, there are relatively few books that focus exclusively on it. This is the first presented in the context of Imago principles and practices. In fact, the book has done us a great good by distilling, in Chapter One, much of the core of Imago into Two Foundational Beliefs and Six Pillars for Building Strong Relationships, which Francine and Bruce developed together over the last five years. The clarity with which she presents these "Two and Six" makes it easy to understand at a high level how putting these into consistent practice will gradually lead us to Peace and Belonging.

The letters that follow, each in its own way, then gives us an opportunity to see in detailed practice how these "Two and Six" represent a real path forward with a high probability of relationship repair and growth. We see practical application in letters to family, to friends and lovers, to siblings, spouses and even employers. We see immediately that Francine lives by what she is recommending by beginning the letters with a deeply felt personal communication to her own aging mother. Many of the examples that follow of are also filled with emotional angst. Yet, with steady, gentle, masterful guidance through mazes of hurt and anger, Francine has provided her clients positive ways to express pain so that the recipients might actually be able to deeply absorb the messages, rather than feel accused or drowned in the writer's hurt, fear and anger. In some cases, this happens with the simple turn of a phrase from an indictment to an authentic sharing of pain. Throughout her process, we see a transition from shadow to light with stunning elegance, creating important openings for relationships to move from hurt to healing.

There is a profound truth that emerges from this work: when relationships spiral into chronic hurt, we are called to create a different way of being in those relationships, one characterized by a devotion to consciousness, empathy, self-reflection and self-correction...one that holds the very real promise of both people in the relationship arriving at a place of genuine Peace and Belonging.

Andrea and Bob Kamm,
Los Osos, California, February 2019

Introduction

Why Letter Writing?

I am a Clinical Psychologist who, over the last 30 years has specialized in working with relationships. This has sharpened my understanding of their inner dynamics.

I have used this knowledge throughout my practice, particularly in helping clients write letters. Clients have thanked me so many times, and reported they learned a lot through my coaching them to write an empowered, assertive note.

Relationship dynamics are a world of their own. Although initially, they may seem incomprehensible and introduce us to a world of chaos – they are not! They are, however, definitely counter-intuitive to one's reactive nature. It is reactivity that becomes dangerous for the health of any relationship.

When I work with a single person on matters that are relational in nature, I often recommend that they communicate with that person through letter writing.

Letter writing?

Yes, letters and, nowadays, emails or texts, are effective ways for two or more hurt or fearful individuals to communicate. When we are hurt we often react and protect ourselves against the hurt by attacking or being dismissive, by explaining and going to great lengths to clear our good name, by being manipulative, trying to induce guilt, pouting . . . or . . . all of the above! That's when the wisdom of letter writing comes in.

In emotional matters, I lead my clients into a calming down period. Sleep, meditation, writing in a journal, going to the gym, doing yoga – whatever works for them and offers a cooling off period. In the midst of reactivity comes more reactivity, in the midst of hurt comes more hurt, and in the midst of humiliation comes a desire for vengeance. None of these paths can bring Peace and Belonging.

So allow for letting steam out, emoting and getting in touch with your anger and your pain. Do that away from the person who hurt you, even if you are planning to never see them again. Hurting someone because you are hurt may feel good temporarily, but only temporarily. On the other hand, learning to write an authentic, heartfelt note can place you on that road to a richer, more connected relationship.

When you write a letter – preferably a brief one – you can choose your words carefully.

Writing a letter allows you to pause as often as you need, to read and re-read out loud to yourself to hear the impact of the words you just wrote. Are they authentic? Are they an honest reflection of what you are experiencing without being hurtful or conveying a judgment and a superior attitude?

On the receiving end, the person can react whichever way they wish. That's a big plus. This person has the right to feel their own feelings, and since you are not in their presence, their reactions can't hurt you. Then later, they can read the letter again and again. They can sleep on it, reflect on what you're saying, and maybe, and hopefully, slowly let it in.

I am hoping you can feel enriched by reading a selection of these letters. Some of them were never sent. They were written strictly for the benefit of the writer. All of them are real, both those received by my clients, or those I helped them compose. I've changed the names and locations to preserve anonymity, but the content has been left intact. Also, I have received permission from each person to include the letters we are using.

Every skill has its set of rules, and writing letters is no exception if you want to accomplish your goal. If your goal is to "get it off your chest", then write freely and privately. Sometimes that is the best first step – a stream of consciousness in your journal to help you regain your balance. I strongly recommend you write and burn letters for release and letting go. You don't send such a letter. It is valuable to you, but would hurt the receiver. Feeling vengeful is a very understandable human emotion. However, we need to learn to clear the slate without hurting others. "An eye for an eye" philosophy will lead us to a life of misery and alienation.

Our goal is "Peace and Belonging".

Chapter 1

Guiding principles for Peace And Belonging

My husband, Bruce Crapuchettes PhD, also a clinical psychologist, and I have had a 30 year practice working with couples. In our work we have identified "Two Foundational Beliefs" and "Six Pillars" of a thriving relationship. We believe they are good guiding principles and will briefly mention them here. For more details see our book, ***"Getting Back The Love We Had"*** *Vol 1 Ch 3* (available on Amazon).

The Two Foundational Beliefs we are convinced are non-negotiable in human relations are:

1. S***ubjective Experience***. Having a different brain and different histories, we will experience the world differently – not better, not worse, *differently*. Coming to grips with that concept will speed up our journey toward Peace and Belonging. You like the beach. I like the mountains. You like movies. I like live theatre. You want more government. I want less. Similarly, we describe situations in opposite ways: You thought I was exaggerating, making a mountain out of a mole hill; I thought you were dismissive and judgmental.

Learning to integrate views that are dissimilar to ours and to accept them without putting them down, is precisely one of the hallmarks of maturity.

2. ***Shared Contribution***: In some way, if there is on-going tension in any relationship, more than one party contributed, otherwise, one party would say, "You're right! I had never thought of it that way." This would abort any

escalation of bad feelings. It requires, of course, that we remain open enough to consider alternatives. Developing the willingness and ability to see how I contributed and "owning my part" without shame or defensiveness is another one of those hallmarks of maturity. Because we know we had good intentions, it is very hard to let in that we still may have hurt someone. *The danger is that it becomes all about our intentions instead of about the net effect of our actions.* Yet many of our actions may have had consequences we had not anticipated. And that, of course, is related to the first Foundational Belief: we experience the world differently. Truth is, if I hurt someone, I hurt someone. Yes, this person may be particularly sensitive, but still I hurt him/her. My search for Peace and Belonging will require that I learn how to relate to this highly sensitive person.

In addition to these Two Foundational Beliefs, we also identified Six Pillars for Building Strong Relationships. They are:

Pillar #1: Assume the Best of The Other

You've got to be kidding!!

Actually, I'm not, I'm dead serious. I believe everyone in life is doing their best under the current circumstances, even when their best is awful. The awfulness of their actions is a reflection of the depth of their hurt and of their lack of consciousness.

In our search for Peace and Belonging, it is important that we receive what another person is saying, even if we disagree, even if we have a hard time wrapping our minds around what they are saying, even if it sounds cruel and awful. Again, at this moment, it is the best they can manage. Put all your energy in not countering or judging what you are hearing. Now is not the right time to share *your* perspective. This is not about you, it is about the other person. This is a concept I will use a lot in the letters I help clients write.

Pillar #2: Assume the Best of Yourself

Believe YOU are a good person, because what is true of your "partner" is also true of you. You are doing your best at this moment even when you do awful things. Learn to embrace your imperfections and stay grounded in your innocence!

This applies to all people in any relationship: not only believe that the other is a good person, but believe at the very core of your being that *you* too are a good person even though you are not perfect. In fact, embrace your imperfections along with the imperfections of those around you – family, friends, or colleagues. We were born with the potential of being good human beings *and* equally imperfect, all equally capable of loving kindness *as well as* equally capable of hurting each other. All hurtful behaviors, those we inflict on others, or those we receive from them, come from feeling hurt and not handling that hurt in a mature manner.

So when someone accuses you of ill intent, don't take the bait. Stay grounded in your innocence. You know you meant well, even if you missed the mark because you're not perfect! Resist the temptation to explain, defend, or apologize. Instead, build this Pillar and embrace your imperfections: “You’re right... I made a mistake... I do feel bad... I will learn to do better...”, and then move on to Pillar #3.

Pillar #3: Contain: Move Away from Reactivity

“Containment” is a word that holds the key to our future “Peace and Belonging”. Containment is the willingness and capacity to hold our emotions in check until the storm has passed so we can practice difficult maneuvers under calmer conditions. Containment is not sweeping a problem under the rug. We’ve all tried some version of, “Let’s pretend it did not happen,” only to have our emotions explode later and do much more damage than if we had dealt with them at the right time and in the right way. That’s why letter writing can be such an effective modality for working through relationship issues. Every word we put on paper can be consciously measured, and our emotional volatility be harnessed and brought under control. Learning to contain is hard stuff. You cannot wish your way to containment. It will require a conscious decision to grow in this area and a commitment to regular practice.

Pillar #4: Own Your Stuff

It takes a lot of containment (Pillar #3) to “own your stuff.”

Because often we are fragile and don’t embrace our imperfections or the belief that we are good people (Pillar #2), we go on the defense. We give explanations as to why we did or didn’t do or say things. We make excuses, saying,

"I didn't mean it that way," "I was tired," or "I was sick." We minimize the impact our behavior has had on the other saying, "You're making such a big deal about it". Because we have not yet become well grounded, we attack the character of the other thereby forgetting Pillar #1, "Assume the best of the other."

Instead of going on the attack, making excuses, or minimizing, stand firm by holding on to Pillar #2 (Believe You Are a Good Person) and then "owning", meaning recognizing and acknowledging that what you did hurt that person. This is different from admitting guilt. Guilt implies you intended to hurt someone. Being a good person and being grounded in your innocence doesn't mean you won't have missteps. It means you accept that you have made a mistake and don't need to go into justification.

Owning your stuff, as difficult as it may be and as much practice as it requires, will strengthen and advance you in your search toward Peace and Belonging.

Pillar #5: Speak from a Place of Authenticity

This requires a lot of wisdom, the wisdom to know to what degree to be authentic in a particular situation. For example, with your boss, or colleagues, it may be wiser to contain, without further action. Just make sure you contain so well that they don't experience you as prickly or grouchy.

Genuineness does not necessarily mean that you say out loud everything you think. *Being authentic or genuine is not a higher value than kindness.* Whatever you say or do, make it your highest priority to choose words that are non hurtful. Notice, I did not say make it your highest priority not to hurt the other. We have no control over whether or not another person will feel hurt. What we do have control over, and are responsible for, are the words we use. This is particularly true when we experience the feeling of anger. Anger is energy, and that energy can easily lead us to behave in a hurtful manner. It is equally true that we can learn to use the energy of anger constructively, such as writing a thoughtful letter which we may or may not send.

Pillar #6: Expect Nothing in Return for Kindness

If you choose to be kind, do it because that's who you want to be. Being kind is not like putting money in the bank where you expect a return. When you show kindness to another human being, do it without a hidden agenda. Keep your loving acts as just that - a practice of showing compassion and empathy because you want to and choose to. That's the person you want to be.

It is important to note that kindness does not mean being a doormat - saying yes to everything. An important lesson for all of us to learn is to be kind and warm while still holding on to boundaries and values that are dear to us. In order to get there, we must differentiate between someone feeling hurt, which we have no control over, and being hurtful through the words we use, and the behaviors we engage in.

These Two Foundational Beliefs and Six Pillars are the principles that guide me when I coach my clients. I think you'll find it useful to refer back to them from time to time as you read through the letters that follow.

Chapter 2

Letters to Family

To bring you into the world of letter writing, I will start with a letter I wrote to my mother on the occasion of her eightieth birthday. I never sent this letter for fear of hurting her. This letter was written for my benefit only. Writing this letter was the beginning of a journey of forgiveness, a major shift in my life at the age of fifty. I began to understand her better, especially the depth of her pain - a giant step toward Peace and Belonging.

As an introduction, I need to say, I hated my mother. It feels awful to write this so bluntly, but it is the truth. Time and again, I cried myself to sleep wishing she were dead. Then when my daughters were around eight years old, she crossed a line that just was too much. I vowed to never, *ever* talk to her again until she apologized. And for five years or so, that is exactly what I did. I was ready to go to my grave in that horrific state of mind.

She was born at seven months in 1915 during WWI. The doctor told her mother, "Don't get attached to her. She will not live." He also told her to wrap her child in cotton and put her in a shoebox. I totally understand that the doctor wanted to save her mother from feeling distressed. I do believe it came from a good place in his heart, but tragically, my grandmother never did become attached to my mother. My mother was genuinely unwanted – in the middle of a brutal war – with a father fighting and dying in the trenches. Her mother was widowed, left alone with three children and filled with anxiety. This is the perfect "no fault" picture. My mother was sent to live far away from her family in the country with her grandparents. At age twelve, she wrote to her mother, "If you don't come and get me, I will kill myself."

It took me a long time to understand the tragedy of my mother's life. Then, when I was about fifty years old, I heard Lewis Smedes (author of *Forgive and Forget* and *The Art of Forgiving*) talk about forgiveness. That one-hour talk totally changed my life. The idea that when the student is ready, the teacher appears became very real for me. I decided to forgive my mother, to focus on the good in her, and to restore her to the human being she was, recognizing that she genuinely was doing her best for what she believed were my best interests.

Dear Mom,

This year, for the first time in twenty-eight years, I called you on Mother's Day. The miracle, however, is not so much that I called you but that my call wasn't motivated by guilt. It was a free, joyful giving of myself. For years, although I may have dutifully mailed you a card, I hated Mother's Day. But it was not only Mother's Day that I hated. I hated you and I hated myself and occasionally my children. I hated the mother you had been to me, and I hated the mother I sometimes was to my children.

Our life together wasn't a pretty picture. You served me a daily diet of yelling and screaming. You ridiculed me. You shamed me in public. You broke my spirit. No words can adequately capture the intensity of my rage. I wanted to scream and scream till I died. Consumed by angry bitterness, I thought you embodied the essence of everything that was evil and I swore I would never forgive you, ever!

For several years, I refused to have any contact with you until <u>*you*</u> *apologized. I wallowed in my pain, nursed my bitterness, and revisited all that is horrible about you, scarring myself more and more, trapping myself deeper and deeper in a vicious cycle of unrelenting hatred. I thought I couldn't let go. And I couldn't. I couldn't because I thought it was* <u>*your*</u> *responsibility to take the lead. After all, you are my mother and you did cause all this pain and you did do all this damage to me.*

Over the years, I started reading and searching and struggling with my life, and I learned that forgiveness wasn't something I would do for you, it is a choice I would make for myself. If I wanted to transform my life, I needed to realize that <u>*my*</u> *life isn't about changing you, it's about changing* <u>*me*</u>*, and it's about changing the way I look at you.*

Today, I am beginning to realize that the abuse I suffered from you was but a reflection of the agony of your own life. But you, you were totally alone. You suffered shame and ridicule, and it is not only that you thought I was a child of the Devil, but you thought <u>*you*</u> *were a child of the Devil. And you had no place to go, nowhere to turn, and no source of comfort. You only had total loneliness and frightening disconnection.*

So today, I cry tears when I think of you, the little girl, so utterly lost in a cruel, inhospitable world. I see your face, your wrinkles. What tragedy do they hide? If you could speak, what wounds would you share with me? What evil forces crushed you so violently that you were never to recover? I don't think I will ever know or ever fully grasp the depth of the agony of your life. I can only guess. But I must never forget that my rage at you was but a shadow of your own rage. The pain you dished out to me was but a reflection of your own pain.

Wayne Muller writes: "Thus family pain broke us open and set our hearts on a pilgrimage in search of love and belonging, safety and abundance, joy and peace that were missing from our childhood story. Seen through this lens, family sorrow is not only a painful wound to be endured, analyzed, and treated. It may in fact become a seed that gives birth to our spiritual healing and awakening."

Nowhere is this truer than for you and me.

So Mom, for the first time in my life, I plan to celebrate you. I am coming over there to Paris in August and am throwing a big birthday bash for you on your eightieth birthday. I am finally free of my anger. I believe you have given me your best and continue to do so. You and I together make an incredible team of survivors!

Thank you, Mom.

Francine

We did go and throw her a big eightieth birthday party in Paris, and we all had such a great time! I have never regretted taking her back into my heart.

Mom came to live with us the last eight years of her life. We experienced a loving and compassionate relationship. The anger and bitterness had been wiped away. She died in my arms on June 9, 2014 (99 years old). This never would have happened if I hadn't written out both my pain and forgiveness in the letter I never sent.

If you choose to forgive, do it in a generous spirit, not out of guilt. If you can't forgive, be accepting and kind to yourself without any guilt. Honor yourself for where you are at, and trust it is exactly where you ought to be for the moment.

Another concept I am fond of while coaching clients, is to start with something positive. Because negativity is what hurts, it sticks to us like velcro and clouds our better judgment. It is therefore important to balance the energies in our lives. Positive energies can be more elusive, precisely because they don't hurt. They do not represent a threat to our survival, so we have to be more intentional in incorporating them in our relationships.

It is in this spirit that I will continue with some personal letters of appreciation I wrote and sent to our family. The first was sent after a family Thanksgiving gathering. The second was a thank you card to my son and daughter-in-law. The third letter is written to my older son after his first wife divorced him.

1. After our 2016 Thanksgiving holiday gathering.

Family gatherings can often be stressful at best. Even if one has negative thoughts and feelings after a family gathering, it is good to send a positive letter thanking members for what you liked. This will go a long way toward having happy times together in the future.

Dec 5, 2016

Dear Family,

It's already been a week since we were together. I look back to this time with great fondness. I want to express my deep appreciation to each of you.

Mishka, you were a kind and generous hostess. Thank you for offering your home. It was the perfect setting. Thank you also to Kodiak and Soleil who were such patient big cousins. They all played so nicely together. Not necessarily an easy task.

Jon and Monica, thank you for coming such a long distance and carving out time from your busy schedule. Dominic and Jon, I thank you for putting your best foot forward, which allowed for the success of our get together. I was in the presence of two grown men who had matured tremendously. I feet very proud of both of you.

Karen, I thank heaven that you joined our family and are the mother of two precious little lives. I will never forget Rachel crossing the "lily pond pool " putting all her might into it, succeeding, and doing it over and over again! She was by far the youngest doing it. Her zest for life is awesome. Neither will I forget Daniel's attempts at roping the calf. He kept going until he made it!

And Mishka, seeing you dance was also a lot of fun as was the lunch at your hospital on Monday. Loved your hospital and how much your colleagues appreciate you. You have accomplished a lot and I couldn't be more proud of you.

These memories are the best present you could ever give me this Xmas. All the pictures and memories fill me with pride and deep gratitude.

Thank you, thank you, thank you.

XOXO

Mom

2. A card sent to our son and daughter-in-law to thank them for holiday time spent together.

Today is a happy day
because of you!
Thanks

Dear Dominic and Karen –

Precious moments were many, but the one that sticks to my mind is the evening putting the terrarium together. Dad is reading the instructions, the children taking turns putting in rocks or dirt, or seeds . . . etc . . . and spraying with water!!!

Mom and grand parents are silent witnesses, just soaking it in. It feels to me, family time at its best.

We are so lucky to feel connected and feel that we belong together.

Through your kindness and generosity, these are the memories you are creating.

Thank you from the depth of our hearts.

XOXOXO

Mom and Dad

3. Here is a letter I wrote to our son after his wife divorced him fifteen years ago.

I include this to encourage you to write a self reflective letter to a child to include the sadness of wishing you had been a better parent at times. Jon has now been married to his second wife for 10 years.

Dear Jon,

Well, she has left you and that which had started as such a wonderful dream, your hopes, your expectations and her making you number one, all of that has come to an end and has now become such a painful nightmare. How my heart aches for you. I see your pain and I feel a lot of sadness, a lot.

My sadness is because I know how much you need someone in your life to be there for you and nurture you and hold you tenderly, and for you to really feel special deep down inside.

I feel so sad that Dad and I were not able to give you enough of that when you were little and needed it so badly. You were the oldest. Others came along and displaced you. One, then two and three and you learned to make yourself small and to avoid expressing your needs because we were busy with other endeavors. I was busy with my schooling, so involved in my own future and my own career and I didn't know how to be attuned to your needs and how to be sensitive to your feelings.

I had no idea what parenting was about. I was raised under the old dictate that children were to be seen and not heard, and if you felt bad, well, tough. It was tough for me too growing up.

It was not bad will.

It was not that I wasn't committed to you. I always have been. It is that I didn't know what love was all about and I didn't have the foggiest idea of what loving my children meant. I didn't know better and I myself was so bruised I couldn't have done any better.

How sad I feel about it all.

How I wish I could do it over again. If you could be my little one again, I would hold you more, I would caress you more, rock you more, especially when you were crying. I would carry you in a sling close to my heart so you would feel my heart beat and know, really know how precious you are to me.

I would let you be more messy, let you track more dirt into the house and leave more dirty dishes. We would have more cereal breakfasts and more McDonalds for dinner just so that I could revel in your being, so I could look into your eyes deeply and let you know how much more important you are than cleanliness or good nutrition and that no time is better spent than time with you, listening to you, laughing with you and being connected with you.

If I could do it all over again, I would savor your presence in my life.

If I could do it all over again!

I can't go back, but I can tell you today how precious you are in my life, how committed I am to hearing you, to listening to you, to understanding your perspective without losing mine. Today I can let you know that you are only a phone call away, day or night, near by and far, I welcome the sound of your voice – always.

No, I can't do it all over again, but I can continue to grow as a person and I am committed to you and to becoming a better mom – all the time.

You have made my life infinitely richer, infinitely softer and infinitely more precious. I never dreamed I could feel so thankful for having you in my life.

I love you,

Mom

4. Next comes a letter from a distressed mom – with a coached response from her daughter.

Susan is one of my clients in her 40's and because she did not know how to answer this letter from her mom, she asked for guidance.

Dear Susan,

I love you from the depths of my heart, but I am terrified of you! 12 years ago my spine collapsed. You assumed everything wrong, including the money. I got MediCal and the state made a large settlement with me because I was so very sick. I have spent most of my days in the hospital or in assisted living nursing facilities. I am not an addict or have never been one. My heart is bad. I have a pacemaker and continuous blood clots. My lungs keep collapsing and I continually have pneumonia. I am on blood thinners. All three of my doctors do not want you around me now!

I am too sick and too horrifically terrified of you right now!! I need time to get better. I don't want to die now!! I hope your life is wonderful and I wish everything wonderful for you!!

I have 3 more surgeries to go. I have had 30 surgeries. Grandma has MediCal too and is well cared for!

I think you get the picture.

Give me time! Don't assume ***please!!***

Please let me get better and don't hurt me!

I love you so very, very much!!

We certainly can understand how utterly distressing and confusing receiving this letter was for my client, especially since it encapsulates the quality of the mother/daughter relationship they have had for as long as my client can remember. Still I believe my client deserves inner peace and, yes, the mother deserves compassion. I believe the two go hand in hand. Here is the letter I coached her to write in response:

Dear Mom,

Thank you for writing to me. You have gone through a lot, especially with your health. So many surgeries and so much pain.

Right now you asked that I give you space. You're saying that's the best thing I can do to help you feel safe. I am absolutely willing to do that. I want you to get better and am committed to contribute to that end as much as I can.

Thank you for reaching out to me.

Love,

Susan

The goal of this letter was to show empathy toward her mother who is obviously in deep emotional turmoil. My client's natural tendency was to simply ignore the letter. But that would have been cold and insensitive. By writing this short note, she is practicing containment at its best, meaning countering her natural tendency to attack and/or withdraw.

5. Here is a coached letter from an angry client to her Dad

Monika had asked for help from her Dad when her husband, Andrew, went into the hospital for serious surgery. He refused. She was furious.

I include this letter to show that it is possible to share negative feelings and remain respectful. This letter was sent and, I believe accomplished this goal.

May 29, 2015

Dear Dad,

I did indeed choose not to respond to your calls. It

isn't so much that I'm angry; it is that I feel hurt. Actually, deeply hurt.

The last words from you that I can hear were, "I'd do anything in the world for you, honey." I did need you the week of June 18. And Ricky, your grandson, needed you. I am in a tender place and still need some time to process.

Andrew is in bad shape. Really bad.

The kids are graduating in a week and there are an exhaustive number of things on our calendar between now and Andrew's surgery.

Please be patient with me. Eventually, I'll get over it.

Love,

Monika

6. Here is a long letter from an angry father with a coached response from his son.

This letter was much too long for this book (many pages), therefore I have shortened it for the sake of the reader. It contains what I believe are many mistakes. I will make some comments at the end.

Dear Brad,

It is time for me to write you another father-son letter.

I believe that you did not mean to be disrespectful and hurtful in this name change of yours. And I do believe you love me. But I think you did not sufficiently think this through; if you did think it through, to me, that is worse, because that means you calculatingly, traded away something of much greater value for something of far less value.

I reject any postmodern, relativistic explanation, that my interpretation of this is merely my subjective interpretation, and you have a different one, and both are valid. Anthropologically, and objectively, though not all, most cultures and most in our culture will view it as an act of dishonorable disassociation from your family of origin. They intuitively know there is some reason why a person is rejecting their family name. For Jewish immigrants who did this, it was to distance themselves from their minority and persecuted status in Europe so they could get a fresh start socially and economically in the New World. They did not want a name that continually identified them with the Jewish ghettoes. I don't believe there is anything at all similar to this in your case.

As far as I can tell, you want to have a more easily pronounceable name for the public, not to have to spell "BJ----------" all the time. And also you, somewhat, want to establish a separate identity from us, for public business purposes.

I am a biblical man, and in Scripture, as you know, names are highly significant; they carry the meaning, often embody the character of the person who owns the name. Our family name identifies us, unites us, carries our memories. It should be a refuge of security and pride.

This is the most unloving thing you have ever done to me and your mother. Do you realize that by doing this, you are forcing your mother and I to explain, with embarrassment, for the rest of our lives, why our oldest son, repudiated our family name?? We will have to say, "Oh, he thought he could make it better in the business world with an easier name."

I experience this as a betrayal. I urge you to return to your better self and values, to think better of this decision and reverse it. If you do not reverse it, the wound, the embarrassment and feeling of dishonor will be there in me until my dying day—that my firstborn son rejected our family name, for unworthy reasons.

Love,

Dad

My thoughts:

Dad used a very common technique, that of trying to shame his son and "guilt him" into changing his behavior. Many parents take that route. The reason it is done so commonly is that it often leads to an apparent success. What it doesn't show, however, is the price one pays, namely, the alienation between father and son. Brad confirmed how angry and affected he was by this letter. He haS many churning negative emotions, which do not enhance the quality of their relationship.

Remember Foundational Belief #1: Reality is a Subjective Experience. At this point, Dad is unable to accept that his son's reality is different from his own. He is convinced that his interpretation is the only correct one, and a priori, rejects that of his son's. I also believe that Dad is mistaken when he writes: *"Do you realize that by doing this, you are forcing your mother and I to explain, with embarrassment, for the rest of our lives, why our oldest son, repudiated our family name?? We will have to say, "Oh, he thought he could make it better in the business world with an easier name."* This feels like a painful put down. No, he doesn't have to explain anything to anyone. He does have to practice Pillar #1: Your Partner (in this case your son) is a Person of Good Will. It will be important for Dad and Mom to give a positive light on their son's behavior. Something like, *"Yeah, it felt to him like the right thing to do. He also found it to be a good business move."* And if the person pushes the issue some more, the father could say, *"Yes, it hurt me at the time, but I am learning to respect Brad's decision, different as it may be from my view."* I would tell Dad to stay on that note - convey that the two of them are learning to be on a different side of an issue, and still remain respectful of one another.

Here is the letter I would have coached the father to write had I been given the opportunity:

Dear Brad,

You have changed your family name and I just want to tell you how hurt I feel by that. It is hard for me not to take it personally and not to experience it as a rejection of me and of your heritage. I am hoping you will be willing to reconsider. That would be a wonderful gift of love to your mom and me, as well as to the extended family.

Regardless of your decision, I know I can work it through and I especially know I love you deeply and that will not change!

Your hurt and loving Dad

As I worked with Brad, here is the letter I helped him craft as a response.

Dear Dad,

First, thank you for letting me know about all the emotions you are experiencing from my change of name. I see that you are attaching many negative interpretations to my decision. It makes me sad that, to you, it means a rejection of my heritage. That must be very painful.

I have no desire to distance myself from our family name, as if there is something wrong with it, or with the people who have it. I absolutely loved visiting the birthplace of my ancestors together, and nothing will ever change my connection to them and their land.

While at some level I would like you to understand where I am coming from, I sense that trying to communicate that to you would feel invalidating, and besides, your feelings would get in the way. All I am asking is that you do not judge me, or my character. I have different standards and different filters than you do. But I am a man of courage and high ethical principles, as are you.

My hope is that we can learn to hold different opinions, yet remain mutually respectful.

Love,

Brad

I recommended that Brad not answer his Dad's letter point by point. That is something he has done many times in the past, each time with disastrous results. It has only kept the fire going and has contributed to a tear in their father-son relationship. At this point, the argument is at an emotional level and responding to feelings with logic simply does not work. It can't. The seat of emotions is in our "old brain", our reptilian brain. Logic comes from our frontal lobes and those two parts of the brain do not communicate well with each other: If we try to convince with reason when we are dealing with feelings, we hit a wall. Then we justify using a jack hammer or a bulldozer to destroy the wall. All the while moving farther and farther away from Peace and Belonging.

Here is Dad's response to this above letter:

October 12

Brad,

I appreciate that you acknowledge I am offended and hurt. But you did not say anything in this letter. There is no content other than that acknowledgement, and your statement that you think it futile to explain your reasoning to me. I disagree. I would understand your reasoning. I would probably disagree, but I would understand. I think you owe it to me to explain. You answered none of my reasoning in my letter to you.

You owe it to me because I'm your father and because at this point I think you have traded something away of much greater value than what you gained. The price for what you think you are gaining is way too high. Read the biblical book of Proverbs...

Dad

In other words, Dad feels that acknowledging that he is hurt is the equivalent of "no content" - a sweeping annihilation of his son's good work. Dad disagrees with the idea that it would be "futile to explain your reasoning to me." Dad has forgotten the long history they have.

With my coaching, Brad chose not to respond in order to avoid feeding an ongoing conflict and a widening gap between them.

I believe this was a wiser choice in the pursuit of "Peace and Belonging".

Whether Dad would understand or not, I don't know. But I do know that Brad does not FEEL understood by his Dad on this issue, as well as many others. Dad said, "You owe it to me because I'm your father." Dad can certainly have that belief, but actually he is only entitled to respect, not just because he is the Dad, but first and foremost, because he is a human being. Dad deserves respect. The novelty here might be that Brad deserves equal respect. I believe that Brad's letter was respectful.

PS: I recently saw Brad. He mentioned that Dad never raised this issue again, and for Brad that's a big step in the right direction. I believe it was to a significant degree, the result of his not having engaged in a point by point power struggle with his dad.

7. A rough draft of an un-coached letter from a father to an estranged 24 year old daughter followed by my comments and a coached letter that I recommended he send instead.

Dear Mary,

I was talking the other day with a friend about raising children, and being a parent, and the joys, and wonder, and rewards, and challenges. And then we started talking about our failings as parents. About things that we, upon reflection, perhaps could have done better.

We talked about how children learn behaviors from us, as parents, and how those behaviors circle around to us. During the conversation, I began to think about all that was going on in my life during your first years – whether that was your first three years, or first five years, or first 10 years, or first 18 – and I thought about how that might have felt to you, as my daughter.

I had so much going on between work, and your sisters, your mom, and projects, and friends, and my own growth – that, many times, I believe that you might have felt that I wasn't present-enough to you. That I was distracted. And, perhaps, for you that might have felt that I didn't care enough, or that I cared more about other people or other things or myself, than I cared about you. If this is your truth – that is, that I was distracted - I wanted to acknowledge it, and open up the possibility with you of dialogue about it.

Love,

Dad

Trying to capture the essence of dad's letter, I would say that it is primarily about *him*. "I had so much going on... I was distracted..." This is probably representative of what Mary experienced when she was growing up. When he attempted to own his stuff, it was tentative "perhaps" or "if that is your truth".

Here is the coached letter I recommended he send instead. I was sensitive to being encouraging and chose to keep the first paragraph which was his. Building good will is essential.

Dear Mary,

I was talking the other day with a friend about raising children, and being a parent, and the joys, and wonder, and rewards, and challenges. And then we started talking about our failings as parents. About things that upon reflection, we could have done better. We talked about how children learn behaviors from us, as parents, and how those behaviors circle around to us.

Thinking about what I could have done better, I wish I had been more emotionally present for you. I wish I had spent more tender moments with you. I wish I had understood better where YOU were coming from.

I didn't know how to do any of that. I am committed to learning. Thank you for giving me the opportunity.

I love you,

Dad

8. An exchange between mother and grown daughter. The first back and forth were un-coached, and then the mother reached out for help, and I coached her final response which brought a satisfying conclusion.

Dec 17

Good morning Donica,

It sounds to me that you are frustrated with me because you feel that I have not been making quality time for you or making you a priority. You said that you think I am too busy to give you my undivided attention. You also told me that since I don't see you very often I was not present for you in the way you needed me to be while you were home. I want you to know that I can own the fact that I have and do sometimes feel distracted and have not been able to give you the attention you deserve. I do regret this. I have said to you that I will be more conscious about this but have yet to make you feel that I am really "getting it" in terms of my behavior.

I DO want you to feel that you are a priority in my life because you are!!

In terms of finding quality time to interact with one another I would like to propose that we predetermine time(s) that we know we both can be available for one another. This will avoid other one of us from feeling slighted. I hope you can forgive my imperfections.

All my love and kisses,

MOM

Dec 17 - same day - this tells us the daughter was quite reactive

(No beginning salutation)

While I appreciate your kind words, you have said these words multiple times without any follow through. Words are worthless without action.

It is an honor and a privilege to be invited into my life, particularly now that I'm engaged. You have disappointed me too many times. So, at this point, I will not

be including you in preparing for my wedding. I will let you know if I want your input, if at all. There are consequences to your actions.

(No ending salutation) - This confirms the daughter is angry.

This is when Mom contacted me to ask for my help. Here is the coached response we worked out together and that she sent.

Dec 19

Dear Donica,

While receiving your e-mail was painful, I am glad that you sent it. It is the kind of feedback that I needed. I have failed you many times, not being really present for you, not focusing on you and what you had to say. I have let my own inner world get in the way and by doing so I have hurt you. I have said words and my actions did not match those words. I agree with you, words without actions feel shallow.

Thank you for giving me the opportunity to self reflect and especially to change and grow just because I love you.

I hope you can someday forgive me my lack of sensitivity. I want to learn to be a better mom for you.

Much as I have loved you imperfectly, I love you deeply.

Mom

Dec 20 - from Donica.

I appreciate you hearing me and for your apology. I hope we can both grow from this experience. I love you too.

My comment on this exchange:

Mom was genuinely attempting to hear her daughter and validate her perspective. What did she write that let us know she missed the mark? Well, she is writing about Donica's experience: "You feel . . ." or "You said that you think . . ." "You also told me . . ." Then Mom wrote she owns those facts, but just the words, "I own the fact . . ." do not convey that she does, in fact, own her shortcomings. Then using words, "I do sometimes . . ." feels like watering down her contribution. Similarly, just telling Donica, "I do want you to feel . . ." , she must actually behave in such a way that her daughter *feels* that she is a priority.

I believe that the letter we wrote together on December 19 accomplished this.

9. The next two letters are from moms who are learning to "own their stuff".

First is a coached letter from a mom to her 25 year-old son that is a good example of "owning her stuff". She is a Jewish mom and her son is dating a Mormon young lady.

Dear Tim,

During your last visit, I "lost it". I raised my voice and "dumped" on you. Over the past few months, tension has been rising in me (a confluence of events) and I eventually reached a breaking point. I do regret handling my emotions the way I did, expressing my negative feelings in a negative way and at the wrong time. I also was blaming my tension on Patricia, but the tension that was building in me was my own.

All this is to tell you I do feel bad about the way I have been handling my discomfort with you dating Patricia.

Timmy, I may be your mom, but I still have a lot to learn and you are being my teacher. You are teaching me tolerance and the true meaning of love.

I love you, and you will never know how precious you are to me.

Love,

Mom

Here is another coached letter from a mom "owning her stuff":

Dear Michael and Kristen,

Dad and I have done a lot of work together with a relationship coach.

As a result, I am coming to realize that I had formed an alliance with both of you against Dad (my coach says the technical term is "triangulation"). *That has been a big problem between Dad and I. The last two times that come to my mind are Father's Day and visiting Grandpa in the hospital.*

I am committed to changing that pattern. It may not always feel good to you, primarily because I will be behaving differently, but I am convinced our whole family will benefit.

Thank you for hearing me.

I love you both
XOXO

Mom

10. Here is a letter from a mom to her son and daughter-in-law. First is her un-coached letter which she wanted help with, followed by a coached letter which she ended up sending.

Here is the un-coached letter:

Dear Robert and Esther,

I write because I have painful feelings still about you and Robert's decision not to let Ken and I have alone time with Ellen, Zoe and Oliver. I had been wondering what was happening this way for years. I didn't understand why arrangements were the way they were and we were never allowed to care for the children. I should have asked years before. Once when I offered to come and help when a baby was born, you said, "It is better for us to have non familial help." Or something similar. Then when you were here at Christmas, it wasn't until towards the end of the visit, that Robert and I had time alone together and I offered to have the children here so you two could have alone time and he said, "Oh we have talked about that," and I said, "What?" We hadn't. I felt something but hadn't understood that at some point you two had made this decision that you did not feel we were safe guardians for the children to be with alone.

I own that we have made a few errors of judgment that were terribly upsetting to you both. Also, I know you feel I have not in the past subscribed as rigorously as you two do, to the wearing of life jackets and seat belts. I would of course do anything you wished me to do, in order to have the joy of being able to have the children here. I feel terrible that you never discussed this with us, nor gave us the opportunity to make agreements with you about how you want things to be.

This is also painful to me because Peter and Karen have since the beginning had times of caring for the children alone. I don't even know how to express the pain of this. The children stay with those grandparents but we are not allowed to. I have sometimes imagined asking you to imagine Robert and you splitting up and your wanting with your whole heart to heal that relationship and have a family together and for four or five years waiting and trying as best you could to restore the connection and love. Then imagine Robert deciding to divorce you and marry another woman. Then imagine Oliver growing up, marrying and allowing Robert and the other woman to care for your grandchildren but not you. I honestly wonder how that would be for you.

Warm hugs,

Leslie

Here is the coached letter that was sent instead:

Dear Robert and Esther,

First, Esther, I want to let you know how blessed I feel that you have joined our family. You are the mother of three lives, so precious, I can hardly tell you. Thank you for your presence in my life.

At the same time, my heart is heavy and I feel much pain with the rift between us. Clearly you have decided that Ken and I are not safe to be left with the children alone. That hurts to the core.

Robert, Esther, I have made mistakes in the past. I deeply regret them and am absolutely wanting and willing to learn from them. I want to learn to do things exactly as you would like them to be done.

I love you and I love your little ones. I want to learn to be a good grand'ma – and Ken as my companion is equally dedicated.

I would like you to give us a chance. I would like to sit down and lovingly and respectfully talk things through. What can I (we) do to gain (re-gain) your trust.

I am eager to hear what I (we) could do, what steps we could take to ease the tension I experience around the grand-children, to right the mistakes I have made, to love you both in the manner you need to be loved.

Warm hugs,

Leslie

I actually do not know whether this letter made a difference. Regardless, it was such a positive step for the grandmother to be willing to send it. She owned that she made mistakes. She does regret it and she asked what she could do to begin the repair work. These steps are impressive to me.

Chapter 3

Letters To Friends And Lovers

1. Kathy and Rob

I am enclosing a string of emails between Kathy and Rob, and between Kathy and me. Kathy is a 28 year-old single female from New Zealand working in Thailand who was feeling overwhelmed by the amount of messages she was receiving from her fairly new boyfriend who lived in New Zealand.

While she enjoyed her relationship with Rob, his texting her every day made her uncomfortable. She felt smothered and didn't know how to tell him that in a manner that would be respectful of herself while remaining kind toward him. She liked him and would have liked to develop a relationship with him. But his constant contacting her was pushing her away. She wanted to set boundaries and pull back some, and was unsure how to do that.

Here is the letter I coached her to send:

Dear Rob,

First let me tell you that I appreciate the attention and kindness you're giving me. I experience you as a true gentleman – and I feel grateful.

At the same time, our relationship is quite new and I sometimes feel a little crowded. I am of course, very concerned not to hurt your feelings but if our relationship is to develop and mature, I need to take the risk and ask you to connect with me less frequently, let's say no more than twice a week.

I am especially concerned that you may pull back entirely and that is not my desire. I would feel bad about that.

I do enjoy our times together and look forward to deepening the connection we have.

Your friend,

Kathy

What happened is that she set her boundaries, which meant she was willing to risk the relationship. As a result, he pulled back entirely, precisely what she had feared. There could have been a different outcome that would have brought them closer together. He could have been grateful that she had kindly let him know that his manner of courting her was pushing her away.

How painful and difficult it is to love the other the way the other needs to be loved!

Three months later he dropped her a note expressing his surprise at her request to text her less often (no more than twice a week). Unsure of what to do, she turned to me for help.

I coached her to write the following letter:

Hi Rob,

It makes sense to me that you were surprised by my note.

You are correctly picking up a change in me. I am learning that I tend to be "co-dependent" and have had a hard time setting my boundaries and sticking to them. Yes, it is very dramatic even for me. But I do believe this is the right course of action.

Thank you for inquiring about me.

With much kindness in my heart,

Kathy

As we kept working together, Kathy got clarity that she did not want to develop a long-term intimate relationship with Rob. Still it was his birthday the next day and she felt obligated to wish him a happy birthday. In addition, she was willing to meet with him in the town they both came from during her visit home. I pointed out to her that this was giving him mixed messages. However, she felt the meeting was an opportunity to achieve closure.

It is not unusual for me to run across this thinking, namely that one has to meet in person in order to bring about a clean, ethical end to a relationship. I disagree with this thinking. In my mind, it only creates confusion and ambiguity. I recommended she write the following letter instead.

Here is the coached letter:

Dear Rob,

You may be surprised to receive this email from me since our communication is very sporadic. I have experienced you as a kind person and I have enjoyed the process of getting to know you better. It is in that spirit of friendship that I am wishing you a happy birthday.

I do not feel ready to envision myself being in a long-term relationship with you. I want to pursue my path and dream, and right now, I realize it does not include a partnership with you. Since I won't be pursuing a friendship with you, I therefore have decided not to see you while I am back home.

Thank you for your time and generosity with me.

This comes wishing you a fulfilling future.

Kathy

Notice that Rob's, not contacting her for three months, was precisely what she had feared. This concretely points to the reality that if you set boundaries for yourself, you may be putting the relationship at risk. *It does not mean it wasn't the right thing to do.* It allowed Kathy to understand Rob better and more accurately evaluate the potential of the relationship.

The above note brought a volley of responses from Rob. Here is what Kathy wrote to me:

Hi Francine

I just received an explosion of messages. I haven't checked my messenger but here is a summary of the ones that came into my email:

Email 1:
Badly played Kathy Badly Played.
After everything?

Happy birthday indeed.
Did you pop a card in the post? Perhaps with a few thousand $ so that I can afford to work through that one with a shrink?

You're. . . I don't know I've just lost faith in all humanity.

Email 2:
Didn't you say – how you end is just as important as how you start, if not more so?

Sheesh Kathy.
You've got some bad jeu jeu coming your way I suspect.

Email 3:
No honestly though. You've fallen in love with me haven't you! That is what this is about isn't it!?

Kathy has fucking fallen in love with me and she can't fucking deal with it.

Bye forever Kathy.

This was my letter to Kathy:

Hi Kathy,

He obviously feels very hurt by your email. Please resist the urge to respond. Have empathy, but don't express it to him. Share your feelings with me or with friends, but not with him. Allow him to have his grieving process and make sure it is away from you. At this point trust the "bye forever". (He will probably break it). But YOU respect it as well as yourself.

Pulling for you,

Francine

Kathy writes:

Thanks for your responsiveness, Francine, and for your guidance. I really appreciate it – it's a confusing time for me.

I understand that he is really hurt and going through his own grief process, which is going from anger to sadness to pleading. I continue to receive messages – is this the point where I just no longer respond? My sense is that he will just continue the dialogue; like you said if there is a crack open in the door he will just keep pushing it open.

Thank you again.

From Francine:

Yes Kathy, I believe it's very important that you don't respond. Your response would be the crack in the door, letting in enough light as to keep his hope alive. If you don't respond he will eventually stop. Your best strategy may be to delete his messages without reading them.

Warm hugs,

Francine

At this point the relationship really ended. This string of emails shows how difficult it can be to end a relationship. It was clearly difficult for Rob to honor her request for less frequent check-ins. That felt so counterintuitive to him. It would have invited him to face his greater fear: abandonment. So he did the very thing that insured that his fear came to pass. Rather than "flow with", he entered into a power struggle. His fears got in the way of the relationship of his dream. Honoring her request was a step he wasn't strong enough to take. He first completely ran away, and then came back with a vengeance.

In our lack of consciousness, that is what we often do - go from one extreme to the other.

2. Christina and Brandon.

Christina is a client who attended our singles group for several years. She had dated Brandon (a church lay leader) for two or three months. Her first sentence to the group one day was, "I think Brandon is manipulating me to have sex." After doing some work together, I encouraged her to send the following coached letter. This is an illustration of holding onto boundaries kindly and firmly while avoiding personal attacks.

Dear Brandon,

There is much about our relationship that I appreciate and enjoy, and at the same time, I experience some discomfort. I would like our relationship to be the same in church, as it is outside of church. What I mean by that is that I would like us to talk to each other in a friendly manner, not "over the top", but not pretending that we don't know each other, which is what you have been doing.

There is a disconnect there for me, so I would like to slow things down and spend more time evaluating where I stand with regards to our relationship. Because of that I would like to forego our date after church tomorrow just to get more space for myself.

What I am hoping to accomplish here, is transparent communication so we build our relationship on solid ground.

I hope you understand.

With much appreciation,

Christina

Brandon broke off the relationship.

When we set boundaries, it is only prudent to expect the other to have difficulty with it. In some cases, as in this one, the person ends the relationship. We should be mentally prepared for this and remember that our integrity is crucial to our achieving Peace and Belonging.

3. Collette and Bernard

Collette and Bernard had been dating each other exclusively and intensively for two years.

At the time Colette came to see me, Bernard was clearly pulling away. He had made previous promises. She now fears he would not follow through.

Here is the letter we crafted together:

Dear Bernard,

I have enjoyed the past week together - loved the restaurant you took us to, loved your companionship, loved our nights together and loved your suggestions regarding my professional quest. I believe we have something special -

although possibly intermittent. While it's not everything I dream, it is good and I am thankful to you.

In the name of our special relationship, I have some favors to ask of you.

- *Would you be willing to continue helping me with my rent through March?* (Just one month away)
- *Would be willing to continue your involvement with the freezing of my eggs?*

Yeah, yeah, I know I'm being daring . . . That's because a man in my life called Bernard told me to increase my self confidence. So, here I am taking risks.

Bernard, thank you for being in my life.

Colette

I don't know whether this note accomplished what Colette was hoping for.

3. Madeleine to Annette and Bill

Here is an un-coached letter one of my clients was proposing to write to her friends. She instead asked for my help before completing and sending it.

This requires a bit of background. My client and her husband were close friends with two other couples. One of the couples used the teen aged son of the other couple to babysit their young daughter. That son abused the little girl sexually. The parents of the little girl confided in my client, under the promise to never tell the first couple (the parents of the teen aged son). My client eventually broke her promise, and for years felt horribly guilty about it.

Dear Annette and Bill,

I am sad to report I have divulged a secret you told me expressly not to tell anyone. I told Bob, and as you know, I had told Laura years ago.

After all these years of listening to our dear friend (Bob) *conjecture in endless looping about what possible reason could exist that his dearest friends* (Annette and Bill) *would cease to be in contact with him was beyond his belief. All he had to go on were dead ends that he must have done something awful, and that Matt and I knew something, but wouldn't discuss it.*

In the end, his suffering did me in. As has your own and your daughter's. Telling Bob seemed to be the only way out for me at that time.

Too, I'm sure, I projected my own fury about being powerless during my molestations onto your daughter's dire situation. And, I apologize for this.

In a few words, I told Bob that the situation was a no-win, he had to move on, and that, maybe his son seems so angry because something happened to him way back when.

Anyway, I don't know anything except I need to apologize to you and to Jenna (the daughter). *This event continues to be an ordeal and a violation of trust and is hurtful to us all.*

And, that Jenna is entitled to be heard, believed, and that I stand with her healing.

That, I am saddened I've hurt your family in this. That was not my intent. That, I consulted with a psychologist I sometimes see, who suggested I write a letter. She proposes, your family be offered an opportunity to say what happened in the presence of the other family. That, this psychologist, or another, as mediator could help both families find a footing toward peace, or else risk the futility not naming the injury and further cycles.

To me, this seems a bit scary to ask, though worthy, in the spirit of Desmond Tutu or Nelson Mandela. That, if you so choose, some good down the road may come of it, maybe helped by the fact that some time has passed and we've all gotten older.

Anything your family might offer the situation would be a great gift to us all.

All my love,

Madeleine

Instead of her letter, here was my suggested letter.

Dear Annette and Bill,

For years I have been haunted by the fact that I betrayed you. It has been on my mind ever since and has left me no respite. After much soul searching – both before I betrayed you, and since – I have decided to come clean and trust that you will forgive me.

I listened to Bob's agonizing questioning as to why his dearest friends had cut him off so abruptly. In the end, his suffering did me in and I told him what had happened to your daughter.

I realize, I was in part taking care of him, but also myself, because of my own agony over the situation, and my inability to carry the weight of holding this secret any longer.

A relationship specialist I occasionally consult suggested I write this letter. It is a scary thing to do, but ultimately lovingly facing the truth is what can set us all free. That includes me, but also you and Jenna and the other family.

Maybe "Truth and Reconciliation" does hold the promise of peace and forgiveness.

I have wronged you by revealing something I had told you I wouldn't divulge. I value you as dear friends and never wanted to hurt you. If you can, please forgive me. If you can't, I do understand.

Thank you for being you and my friends for four years.

Love,

Madeleine

So what was I looking for in the coached version of this letter?

One, the person who is writing, Madeleine, knows what happened. I didn't think it was valuable to go over it again at this point. Giving all the details could come across as defensive. I wanted to stay away from that.

I wanted to make sure the letter was not about giving some unasked for advice, but instead, stayed focused on: *"I betrayed you and I feel bad about it. I want to come clean and ask for your forgiveness."*

Whether Annette and Bill do forgive, that's up to them, and they never have to tell Madeleine what happened for them after receiving the letter. The letter is strictly for Madeleine to make amends in the spirit of these words: "That which is not repaired, will be repeated."

Whether or not Bill and Anette's request of Madeleine was fair and integrous remains an open question.

I do not know the outcome of this letter. After sending it, Madeleine emailed me and said:

"I see my first letter was more self righteous and advice driven, less an apology, which maybe is related to

being angry about my being in this awkward position. The saga continues. I wonder if I'll ever get this. Thanks again!"

Chapter 4

Letters To Siblings

The following letters are between Miriam and Lilly, two sisters who have had a very tense relationship over the past few years. John is Miriam's husband. I have seen them as a couple for several years.

The initial letter from Lilly was very long (over 14 pages), so I have edited out most of it.

Here is the first part:

Miriam,

Being a keen observer, I am sure you have sensed that both Papa and I (and partially Phil) have not embraced John. I want to let you now why we have been less than enthusiastic about him.

. . . (I have edited out many pages here of detailed criticisms of their visit together)

All four of us have separate upbringings, grew up in different countries, different cultures with different values and beliefs. Yet, YET, we all felt it was inappropriate and disrespectful behavior from both of you, especially John. No, we do not have any issues with public display of affection, but to have his hands all over you? Touching you everywhere? Groping you? In front of your own father? Have his parents not taught him anything? Phil was flabbergasted. He said that maybe with the exception of teenage parties (where hormones are raging), he has never seen that before, and he is from Paris!! Eight pairs of eyes do not lie!!

. . .

The letter continues with several more pages of critical judgments. Had I been Lilly's coach, here is what I would have recommended she write instead of the above:

Dear Miriam,

It was nice seeing each other for a whole week, as this does not happen too frequently. Strengthening our family bond is something I value highly, so I was pleased that we had the opportunity.

As I reflect on our time together, I occasionally experienced some discomfort. When we meet next, would you and John be willing to limit your public display of affection to holding hands and maybe an occasional peck on the cheek. I would very much appreciate that and would feel very respected by both of you.

Thank you in advance.

Much love to you both,

Lilly

But this is not the letter Miriam and John received.

What they received was 14 pages filled with criticism. Consequently, their natural tendency was to want to defend their perspective and go on the attack. I strongly recommended against doing that, as it would only fuel the fire of attack/counter attack (my clients had done that in the past). Nothing constructive can come from such a strategy (as my clients had discovered). Instead, I recommended that they "own their stuff", and begin working on what they can change.

Based on these principles, here is their coached response to this first part of Lilly's letter.

Dearest Lilly:

Thank you for once again taking the time to write such a long letter. I do take it as a sign, as you say, that you love me, care for me, and you're looking out for me.

Thank you for caring for me, that's very sweet of you. At the same time, John and I would like to tell you where we're coming from. We have been studying and practicing personal relationships' skills quite a bit. We are learning that love means to love the other the way the other needs to be loved. We can see that both John and I have not been good at that up to this point. We both regret it, and we both want to learn to love you and the family better.

Similarly, we would like you to love us the way we need to be loved. Lilly, it would mean a lot to us that you realize that we do see things very differently; and when we do, we would like to treat each other with respect. Please don't get me wrong, we're not saying we've done a good job of treating you with respect, but we are committed to learn and do better. Conversely, we would like you to avoid bringing in so many events from the past. It feels critical and judgmental to both of us. And it makes it hard to enroll our goodwill.

Thank you, Lilly, for reading this, for your concerns, and for loving me.

At another time soon, we shall address the rest of your letter.

Love,

Miriam and John

Note that I did *not* address the specifics of what actually happened. Finding who is right and who is wrong can only fuel the fire of disconnection. Nothing is to be gained through fact finding; we are not a court of law. What is important is to address the hurt feelings in a manner that remains respectful to all parties involved, and make a commitment to change behaviors.

Lilly's letter continued with many more criticisms and unasked for advice. I have eliminated most of it. Had I coached Lilly, this is what I would have recommended she write:

Dear Miriam,

While I enjoyed much of our time together during this last visit, I also experienced anger, and I don't want to dwell on my anger. That is not good for my own personal health and it's not good for our relationship. Because our relationship is important to me, I don't want to let negativity fester in me. I felt angry when John did not participate in the overall dinner preparation or clean-up, or when he did not share the wine in a way that felt fair to me, or share the cost of the dinner out. While I recognize these are my issues, those issues were triggered by some of John's behavior.

I look forward to spending more time together and would like to ask both of you to be sensitive to who we are and responsive to our sense of equity.

Thank you for hearing me out. I feel better not holding that against you and John.

Love,

Lilly

Many, if not all of the difficulties and tensions in relationships are because of poor boundaries. In this letter there has been a lot of speaking behind each other's back and a lot of "he said, she said, Papa said..." This way of conducting relationships is doomed to failure. Learning to speak for one's self, sharing what one is feeling without negatively analyzing the character of the other is really the task of learning good boundary setting.

After many pages of criticisms, Lilly's letter ends with sending Miriam her expectations for the future. She gives a long list of seven demands as to how both Miriam and John "should" behave which I haven't included. Lilly clearly acts as the person who knows best and expects others to see things her way.

. . . Lilly's letter continues...

I am fully aware I am not going to sit in your good book for speaking my mind. In the past I have not spoken up, about your past relationships, for fear of your anger and the terror you release, but there were plenty of times when I should've. I regret not doing it. I am weary of relationships you get into. I've NEVER trusted any of the men you have dated or married. And I had plenty of reasons not to and unfortunately, I was right... That bloody scares me. I do not trust John and I am wary of him.

Also, both of you need to understand, when you get married, you are not just marrying each other. You are also married into the family. The marriage comes with each other's family. It doesn't matter that we don't see each other often, it doesn't matter that we are not there to witness the every day interactions. We are here, we have the right to speak, to be concerned, and we have the right to "beat the shit" out of John so to speak if he ever mistreats you. We also have the right to give you Miriam an earful if you are unkind to John. We are fair and reasonable people, and most of all Papa, Phil and I all consult each other when there's a concern just to make sure all bases are covered, and all perspectives that we can think of are considered. We are not here to side with only one of you. We are here to root for your happy life, and confront whoever is not doing right.

The seriousness of the lack of healthy boundaries is so clear here. No, by marrying a family member, one does not marry the family. And no, they do not have the right to speak. Be concerned, yes, but they have to learn a different way to share their concerns.

Below is the letter I coached Miriam to send.

Dearest Lilly,

I do want to thank you for being concerned for my wellbeing and my happiness.

The way I think I would experience your love and concerns for me would be to tell me things you like about me, things you do appreciate. I am not so angry, in fact, I don't think I am angry at all, as much as I am overwhelmed by the amount of negativity, criticism and shaming, and I am surprised that you call that unconditional love. My definition of love these days is to love the other the way the other needs to be loved. I would like you to be softer, gentler with me, and speak to me with kindness and compassion.

Yes, I do have my frailties, and yes I have made mistakes. Even though I am on a spiritual journey of growth and healing, still, I will slip. And I would like to be uplifted with respect and compassion. I myself have tried very hard to do this for you, Phil, Papa, Annette, and Maddie, and I will continue to strive for that.

Love,

Miriam

Because so much in the letter was about John, he wanted to respond also. Here is his coached response:

Dear Lilly,

Wow, I don't know where to start. The degree of judgment and unkindness toward me is enormous and I am very uncomfortable with you telling me what to do. I find that demeaning.

I am committed to being kind, respectful, and tolerant of our different perspectives. Lilly, I hope you can do the same for me.

By marrying Miriam, I am not marrying her family. But you are all in my circle now. I hope we can hold one another up with high regard and with the kind of love Jesus would be proud of.

My best to your family,

John

Because this is a very religious family, he wanted to reference Jesus.

Here are the last coached letters in this long series - one from Miriam and one from John.

Dearest Lilly,

You have taken a lot of time and put a lot of thought in your letter. You have pointed out that I was insensitive about inviting you to the wedding. How right you are. How could I possibly even begin to know how difficult it is to travel with two young children! Not to mention Papa. And you rightfully are pointing out the costs involved.

You are right I let my own desire to have you and Papa around at the wedding, guide my request, without looking at the whole project from your perspective. I regret it, and I hope you can forgive me.

I think we can both benefit from us writing to each other, and so, I look forward to more communication between us.

Thank you for loving me, and I hope you trust I too love you the best I know how.

Your loving,

Miriam

Here is John's coached response:

Dear Lilly,

Since you cc'd me, I want to join Miriam in letting you know that I want to learn to respect you fully in the way that makes sense to you. I now understand that inviting you was not respecting you and was insensitive to all that it would have entailed for you.

My heart is open to learning. Thank you for opening my eyes.

John

My focus in these three letters, is primarily on not being defensive. That is obviously very hard to do, but more easily accomplished thanks to the passage of time and having a coach. They are also focused on trying to validate the perspective of the sender, Lilly, in this case. I want to clarify that validating does not mean agreeing. We often mix the two concepts. It is easy to think that if I validate someone, it means I agree. Because we often blur the distinction between validating and agreeing, we often find it excruciatingly difficult to validate someone we disagree with.

Yet I believe it is do-able and it is the road to Peace and Belonging.

Chapter 5

Letters To Spouses

1. Jocelyn and Frederic

Here is a letter from a wife to her husband sent many years ago in 2002 before she had received coaching in the Foundational Principles and the Six Pillars of healthy relationships (see Chapter 1).

I have deleted much of the letter because I felt it was too long for this book. Here is the shortened version:

Dear Frederic,

THIS HURT ME!!

STOP HURTING ME!

STOP HURTING ME!

STOP HURTING ME!! DO YOU GET THAT?!!!

FREDERIC, STOP HURTING ME!!!

And do not mask this – or devalue this with your bullshit excuse, "Oh this is just a reaction she's having from her family history."

I am not!!

This is very real and it's all about you!! It's about you shirking your responsibilities and not growing up! And for whatever the reason is (fear), YOU need to fix it and you need to fix it fast!!

I cannot continue in this relationship where the life in my soul is sucked out of me! Your fear is killing me and it's killing this relationship. You are killing it. Stop killing it!!

I cannot continue a relationship with someone who lives in fear. And someone whose fear prevents and stops him from living the life he wants. I can not continue this – it sucks the life out of me. It makes you needy, clingy and a child – a little whiny boy in this relationship and that's why I have no interest in any type of a sexual relationship. Why would I want to make love with a little boy? That's sick!!!

I want to live with a man – a man who is able to live in this world and uphold and embrace his responsibilities. And no, you have not been doing that for a long time. I really want our marriage to survive, but it can't if you don't change. I know you have the power to change. And I hope you do change.

. . . (a section eliminated)

Frederic, I do love you, but I do not love you unconditionally. Let me repeat that: I do not love you unconditionally! You are hurting me and I do not love someone who hurts me irrespective of whatever the non-intentional rationale may be.

Our marriage is hanging on by a thread – but I believe the damage you have caused can be repaired and I am willing and want to give this one last chance. You need to be in a state where you are in love with life and not in fear, are working full time in some job that generates income, and be working toward your goals by Dec 30, 2002. That actually needs to happen before then, but Dec 30th will be the set date to evaluate if you've turned yourself around.

. . . (a section eliminated)

Frederic – you need to face your fears head-on and win. You – the real vibrant you needs to finally come out and take control of your life. The real you and I've seen glimmers of it on brief and fleeting occasions. It is truly a beautiful thing, and that's why I'm able to give this one last shot.

. . . (a section eliminated)

Please make that happen, Frederic. I'm not asking you to be perfect, Frederic. I'm just asking you to be a man and not a boy.

That is really it – and you need to know that in no uncertain terms! Stop hurting me! Please change! Save our marriage!

Jocelyn

Here are some of my thoughts:

We feel the pathos of this letter, the heart felt pleading, the agonizing request for something to change, the deep desire to save the relationship. It's all there.

Years later when Jocelyn and I started working together, and after hearing the letter read out loud to her, she said, "Oh my God! Nothing has changed. I could have written this yesterday."

Nothing has changed. Nothing different has happened and it has been 14 years. It certainly begs the question: Why?

I like the following concept: *You may not like the principles of the psyche, but you will be subject to them, and your life will be impacted by them.* If you don't follow them, you will pay the price and not get the results you had hoped for. It's like gravity. Whether you believe in it or not, you are still subject to it. Not following sound psychological rules will give you the relationship of your nightmares and not foster Peace and Belonging.

So in this case, what are the principles Jocelyn did not follow, simply because she did not know them? It was not for lack of trying. She was desperately trying. The problem was the way she was going about it. She was asking him to change and threatening him if he did not. She thought all the responsibility lay on *his* shoulders, that only *he* could fix the situation.

That is the polar opposite of how the psyche works.

She had to decide for herself what her bottom line was, and then have a plan, in case he didn't change. She not only needed to have a plan, she had to follow through with that plan. The concept is: "Let there be change in my relationship and let it begin with me."

All relationships exist in a balanced system, like a scale. If you put a little more weight on one side, it will create an imbalance. Either Jocelyn is worth it to Frederic, in which case he will change in order to protect the relationship, thus re-establishing the balance, or she is not, in which case he will not change. It is also possible that she indeed is worth it, but he has learned that she doesn't have enough inner strength to follow through. Her words, then, become empty threats.

Actually, that describes exactly what happened. She had turned her power over to him. She thought only *he* could fix the situation. She came from a place of powerlessness. That is why she did all the pleading and shaming, and told him what to do, "You need to fix it fast."

When we feel disempowered, we use all those techniques – begging, screaming, shaming, threatening or moralizing ("You need to face your fears"). When we come from a place of disempowerment, we turn things around ("You have to let me go").

In fact, it is quite the opposite. She needs to lovingly face the situation she is in, and be willing to let him go. She has to risk all to gain all, but there is no guarantee. She has to be worth it to herself and take action if he crosses her bottom line and contrary to what she told him, "It's something only *you* can do", she is faced with something only she can do.

Reality can be overwhelming, at least initially. It certainly was for Jocelyn. But she is slowly gaining strength. She is more and more willing to challenge herself, increasingly bringing into balance the idea of respecting him as well as respecting herself.

Fourteen years later, after we started working together, here is the letter we crafted.

Dear Frederic,

Our love story started beautifully 21 years ago. The most visible heritage of our love, is our three amazing children. They are a living proof of the loving energy that once existed between us – loving energy that I no longer experience. I do feel awful about that. The goal of my letter is my attempt at re-connection and at re-building what we once had. Our love and our family are precious to me and I want to "fight" for them. But I want to fight a good fight, not something that would tear us apart even more.

Here are three things I would like you to do that would go a long way toward helping me feel loved and respected by you.

First, within the coming month, I would like you to get a job. Any job is fine with me. (Flipping burgers or gardening is ok.)

Second, as long as you don't have a job, I would like you to be responsible for cooking, laundry and grocery shopping.

Third, if you don't have a job in three months, I would like you to move to our back house.

This comes with all my love and deep commitment to our family.

Jocelyn

Jocelyn sent this letter. She waited the three months, he still did not have a job and therefore she asked him to move to their back house, which he did.

2. George and Mary

Here is a letter I received from the husband of a couple I was working with.

The husband was quite new to couples work and had not yet integrated the Foundational Beliefs and the Six Pillars of a Conscious Relationship. I believe it will be instructional for you, to once again, experience what it looks like before and after we are strong enough to put those concepts in practice.

He wrote me:

"After over a month I decided to come back to bed with Mary. I had found her smoking in our backyard and I hate the smell of cigarettes on her breath. I had told her many times that I didn't like her smoking and that I would sleep in a different bedroom if she did. She had agreed to stop.

Rather than welcome me back last night, she said, 'Oh, you're back. The problem is that I have a cold and you might catch it. So I'm not sure that this is a good idea.'

I was furious. I make an effort and decide to come back to please her and that's how she receives me? She wasn't appreciative, only distant and superior. I feel hurt, angry and stuck. Frankly, I find her rejecting and refusing to work with me and my goodwill, my vulnerability and my willingness to come back. I don't see much hope and wish she would just move out!"

This email is rich in lessons for all of us. The writer was not yet strong enough to build any of the Six Pillars of strong relationships. I find that he does not come from a place of self-reflection, but rather one of attack and criticism of his partner. Nowhere does he wonder about what he did that contributed to the current conflict in their relationship. That violates the Foundational Belief that *both contribute to the tension in their relationship* (see chapter 1).

The email also exhibits a lack of containment, meaning the absence of Pillar #3: *"Contain: move away from reactivity"*. Since the writer wrote to us and copied in his partner, it feels to me the email was an attack on her character and motives. Exercising containment would have been to say nothing verbally or in writing until the next session, or perhaps schedule an early, extra session. At any rate, good containment means the other does not know you're containing because you're doing such a good job of it.

Also, George did not assume the best of his partner: Pillar #1: *"Assume the best of the other"*. In fact, he gave the worst possible interpretation of her behavior. He wrote she was distant and superior. I believe there are other interpretations of her behavior.

In addition, nowhere in this email is George *"owning his stuff"* (Pillar #4). He portrays himself as good personified and her as bad and superior.

My experience in reading this email, is one of judgment and blame where I would have liked to have seen compassion and gratitude.

"She wasn't appreciative," he wrote. Well, I don't know. Maybe she was genuinely concerned that he would catch her cold. He is forgetting the other Foundational Belief: that *reality is a subjective experience.* Her reality is different from his. I am not observing much self-reflection in this email. The writer's self-reflection is about <u>his own</u> generosity of spirit, as expressed in the words *". . . my goodwill, my vulnerability and my willingness to come back."* Lastly, he expresses criticism, judgment, and expectation of "goodies" in return for being back. He came back to the bedroom with a hidden agenda – a quid pro quo. "I'm back in the bedroom, so you're supposed to react with gratefulness!" – violating Pillar #6. This strategy is more

likely to create anger and rebellion, whereas we want Peace and Belonging.

So instead of the email above, here is the email I would have liked him to have written (to her rather than to me):

"I moved out of the bedroom five weeks ago because I found you smoking and you had said you would quit. Upon reflection, I regret that. I'm guessing it must have felt punitive to you. I don't want to punish you. I want you to know how grateful I am to have you in my life. Even if you make a mistake and do things I don't like, I do believe in you and in your goodness. I am ready to work through the smoking issue together and come back to our bedroom. Is that ok with you?"

Writing these words would have shown vulnerability, conveyed a belief in shared contribution to the problem (she did smoke and he did react punitively), shown self-reflection and a willingness to own his part and assume the best of his partner. His returning to the bedroom would have been truly a gift of love without expecting anything in return. But to be able to write all this *takes a high level of relational skill that only comes after several years of day-in and day-out practice.* He was still new at it.

Yes, this is tremendously difficult work, yet, which is the better path to choose - continuing to struggle with and hurt each other, or devote ourselves to gradually renewing our way of connecting so that Peace and Belonging are actually attainable?

3. Brigitte and Gary – ownership and regret

One of my clients had a disastrous night at their friend's dinner party. Here are the letters I recommended, focused on owning one's mistakes, the first to her husband, and the second to their friend.

Dear Gary,

I drank too much and then behaved badly the other evening. Consequently, I shamed you in front of our friends.

I regret that very deeply. I regret hurting and humiliating you, the man I love. I hope that eventually you will find it in your heart to forgive me.

I want to learn to love you well.

Brigitte

Here is the letter to the friends.

Dear Teresa and George,

Again, thank you for your lovely hospitality the other evening. I drank too much and I feel I did not honor your kindness in a way that I am proud of. Instead, I humiliated my husband and put you in an awkward situation. I feel really badly about all of that.

Please accept my apologies.

Brigitte

4. Working with a single person who is separated from his wife

When working with a single person when the partner does not want to come to joint sessions, it is imperative to focus on the person present in the room and *that* person's contributions to whatever tension permeates their relationship. It is equally imperative that the client know that just because s/he is the only person in the room does not mean that they are the only one responsible for tension in the relationship. Clients tend to make it *all* of their fault or *all* of their partner's fault. Over and over again, I have had to insist that each person is 100% responsible for their 50% contribution. The task is now, to clearly and specifically see what is *my 50% contribution.* The Basic Principles and the six Pillars are just as relevant working with a single person in a relationship, are just as helpful to the client and help keep the therapist on more neutral ground, rather than "taking the side" of their client. In those situations, I like to use letters or emails. It bears repeating that this practice gives the sender time to focus on every word, making sure they are non-inflammatory and it gives the receiver full permission to be reactive, in the privacy of their home. The sender and receiver can read the letters or emails over and over again if they need to. Corresponding with each other this way, markedly decreases the possibility of the sender and the receiver hurting each other and letting things get out of control. It also eliminates the issues of tone of voice and rate of speech, which may convey judgment and anger.

Here are five letters from these sessions:

Letter #1

The couple was separated and the goal of this first letter was for him to transcend his desire for vengeance. He thinks he understands a lot more about relationships now, and he would like to practice with his wife the many things he has learned and continues to learn in our work together.

Dear Sweetheart,

Here we are, September 1, 2015. Four years ago, we were filled with love and anticipation. Today, my heart is heavy with pain and the very real possibility that my dreams with you will never come to fruition.

We have both hurt each other, and I choose to let go of those hurts. I have chosen to remember the many good times I have experienced with you, and I believe we can work through our difficulties.

I would like to have you by my side as I live my life. I would like to cherish and care for you for the rest of my life. So I ask that you think about you and me making a fresh start—a new beginning toward a fulfilling, loving relationship - a totally new marriage.

I believe in us. I believe that we have great potential.

This comes with an aching heart and all my love.

Michael

Letter #2

This letter exemplifies how to set a boundary, how to own one's dark side, and how to make a direct request.

Dear Sweetheart,

I am appreciative that you want to meet with me again. I want to meet again because I would like to work on our marriage, and I do believe I have a lot to work on. However, a meeting between just the two of us would feel pointless to me because I have nothing more to say right now. So rather than meeting alone tomorrow, I would like to invite you to meet with me and my counselor. I believe she could guide us out of the impasse we are now in.

I hope you believe that there is nothing I would like more than to create a loving, fulfilling marriage for both of us by becoming more conscious of each other's needs.

Love,

Michael

Letter #3

In this letter, we learn that Michael did meet with his wife in a coffee shop. He continues owning his contributions to tension in the relationship, and he affirms his new boundaries regarding money. He had a history of always paying for everything out of guilt, including three adult children, one of them being hers from a previous marriage.

Dear Sweetheart,

Thank you for initiating our last meeting. I enjoyed seeing you. I have loved you and still do, and I have loved you poorly. I can see now that I have been controlling. Being controlling was never my intention, but inadvertently, I missed the mark and I hurt you.

Regarding money issues, you may be surprised at my new way of handling money. Specifically, I am working on my codependency issues with regards to money.

I can imagine that your life has been difficult this past year. My heart does ache for you because I love you. My love is still yours and I would welcome the opportunity for us to learn to become each other's healers.

With all my love and so much more,

Michael

Letter #4

Here, Michael is owning his contributions to the marital discord (Pillar #4: "*Own Your Stuff* ").

Dear Sweetheart,

I was thinking about the ways in which I have hurt you. I want you to know that I hurt you not because I didn't love you or didn't want the best for you, but because I didn't know any better. Whatever I did that ended up hurting you was still out of the goodness of my heart. No matter how good my intentions, though, if I hurt you, I hurt you. I want you to know I deeply regret that.

With all my love,

Michael

Letter #5

In this letter, Michael owns his contribution to the problems and accepts what is, as it is becoming more and more apparent that his wife is not open to working on the marriage.

Dear Sweetheart,

I just want to thank you for writing me back because I believe communication is the only way we can unravel the dynamics between us. I like that you said, "I want to be seen," because I can see that in our lives together, I have not been very good at that and my response to tension was often silence and withholding. I regret that. I didn't know any better. I still have some hope that you will give me the opportunity to show that I can learn to handle my emotions differently. I will, however, accept what is.

You wrote, "Now I believe in me." That makes total sense to me, and I liked reading that. Similarly, I also am learning to believe in myself, which for me means disengaging from the codependent ways of relating that have been the hallmark of my life. That is what you call "some rule of principle I had established." This new behavior is not arbitrary; it is to enhance my own personal growth.

I love you, and I hope you can understand where I am coming from.

Michael

I am sad to report that this couple is now divorced and my heart is heavy, believing that had they come earlier, this marriage could have been saved. They came too late, a common situation with couples, and only once while together. Too much water had gone under the bridge. Once that hurt was too deep, it became the only reality that she could see. The marriage had reached the point of no return.

5. **A coached letter from a husband to his wife after a classic fight around the holidays. They have been married five years. In this letter, he owned his stuff and apologized for it.**

Dear Polly,

I was reflecting on the fight we had on Christmas eve.

Upon reflection, I can see that I escalated the fight by raising my voice and yelling. I would like to learn to hold my ground without raising my voice. I do regret the way I did it and just want to let you know that.

Thank you for being in my life to help me stretch and grow.

Love,

Sam

Chapter 6

A Letter To An Employer

1. This letter is from a 30 year old single lady who works for an NGO overseas.

Dora feels that the management who is phasing out her job, is trying to push her to resign because they don't want to give her severance pay. She feels upset about that and does not know how to proceed.

The goal of this letter is to get more clarity as to what "they" are offering her. The bylaws stipulate that if the new job is 30% or more different from her current job, then she would be allowed to quit on her own and still be eligible for severance pay.

Here is the letter we composed together to mail to her manager.

Dear Josh,

Thank you for our conversation Friday. I am grateful for your appreciation of my work and your sensitivity to my position.

As I told you, I have not made a decision. That's because I want my decision to be measured and well thought out, and I have a few more questions.

I do appreciate the description of what my new position would look like. I would like some clarification on the following:

1. Does the job description I have developed, accurately represent what my new position would entail? Meaning, was I accurate in my understanding of my new responsibilities and focus areas?

2. What would the transition process from one position to the next look like? What are the concrete steps that I would need to take?

3. The new job description seems to be markedly different from my current focus. My understanding is that, it being more than 30% different, I would need to apply for the new position. Am I correct on that?

4. If I am correct, is the new position opened to other applicants?

Thank you in advance for your consideration. I look forward to the clarifications I need.

With kindness,

Dora

Because Dora's letter was not pushy, but was instead direct, clear and kind, they were able to come to a mutually satisfying agreement.

Chapter 7

Epilogue

Relationships run into trouble because of a deficit of understanding and compassion. We need a new process and a new language. Some letters in this book may be surprising in their commitment to embrace gentleness and refrain from aggression. It is my hope that by the end of the book, it is clear that stepping away from the tit for tat dynamic, the authors of the letters remain dignified, strong, and well anchored.

I just helped a mother last week text a clear, loving and firm message to her 29 year old son to leave the house by 7:00 pm or she would call the police. He did move out. She did not need to call the police, and here is the self-reflective feedback she sent me today:

"What I have learned....

I have learned that I have a pattern of not being clear with others with what I want. I then become frustrated and get very angry with them. I describe it as having a long fuse with an explosive ending. I have ruined many relationships in my life with this behavior

I have learned that it is very hard for me to hold boundaries. I am often "too nice" but the truth is that it feels very uncomfortable and vulnerable to ask for what I want. I often don't know how to be clear and I am confused on how to respect myself. People around me know I'm a pushover unless I'm mad. Then they are afraid of what might happen."

This self-reflective paragraph exemplifies several of the points I have made throughout this book, for example:

- speaking with clarity and directness
- being vulnerable
- maintaining self-respect and dignity
- setting and holding boundaries
- avoiding the pendulum swing from passivity to explosiveness
- learning to contain

I would like to end with a story I love. It is a true story, and I believe it encapsulates what Ive tried to convey.

For most of my life I have lived in Southern California and for most of my life I have eaten breakfast outside on our patio just next to nature. It was an amazing setting and an idyllic situation until one day, an entire colony of bees flew by and settled on our property. Our breakfasts were ruined with bees all around us.

I bought traps and more traps. They were hanging all over the property. Bruce, my husband, told me that my strategy would not work because the queen bee will simply produce more eggs to keep the hive thriving.

He was right. I felt defeated.

Then I remembered what Harville Hendrix (author of *"Getting The Love You Want: A Guide For Couples"*) said during my training with him in Imago (the form of couple's coaching I do) that our task is to coach couples to "make friends with the enemy". Those words kept buzzing (pun intended) in my ears: *"Make friends with the enemy!"*

So I told Bruce I was changing my strategy. We were going to make friends with the bees and invite them to our breakfast table. We put a plate on the table - just for them! Through trial and error we discovered what they like best. *They don't like honey, they like meat!* - Costco roasted chicken the best! We also discovered that we had to put their plate on the table about 15 minutes before we sat down to eat.

The miracle did happen. The bees gathered on their plate and stayed there and we enjoyed our breakfast in nature once again.

I often remind myself of that experience in my life. It actually was life transforming. All these letters I have helped clients craft are a practical and real application of that principle.

If you are willing to learn to make friends with the person you perceive as the enemy in your life, you stand a much better chance of achieving Peace and Belonging.

About the author

Francine C. Beauvoir, PhD, is a licensed psychologist who specializes in working with parents, couples, and singles who want to be in relationship. She has written the popular book, *"Raising Cooperative & Self-Confident Children"* and has an audio tape set with the same title. She has trained extensively under Dr. Harville Hendrix in New York and is Certified by The Institute For Imago Relationship Therapy in New York City (1-800-729-1121) as an Imago Relationship Therapist, Workshop Presenter, and Clinical Instructor. She is an experienced educator and trains and supervises psychotherapists. She received her Ph.D. from U.S.C. and is a member of the American Psychological Association.

She is in demand as a speaker, is co-founder of the Pasadena Institute For Relationships, California, where she has been in private practice for 26 year, and has been married for over fifty years with Bruce Crapuchettes, PhD, also a clinical psychologist. Together they have four adult children and seven grandchildren. She and her husband retired in 2017 and now live in Paris, France. Francine still sees clients in person and also via Skype.

She can be reached via email:
francine@pasadenainstitute.com

Website: www.pasadenainstitute.com

Made in the USA
Lexington, KY
22 May 2019